BONES

BONES

POEMS BY MIKE FREEMAN

BIBLIOPUNK PRESS
2007

Library and Archives Canada Cataloguing in Publication

Freeman, Mike, 1967-
Bones / by Mike Freeman.

Poems.
ISBN 978-0-9730688-3-2

I. Title.

PS8611.R435B65 2007 C811′.6 C2007-906459-0

Book and cover design by Kristin Whiteley
Cover photograph (Starling Skeleton) by Simon Battersby © Dorling Kindersley
Author photograph by Krista Ellis

Published by Bibliopunk Press
Toronto, Canada
www.bibliopunk.com

CONTENTS

For Kyle

GRAVITY ZERO

She rose up into the air and the jilted earth let out a sigh.
She rose up and the almond scent of her skin filled the breeze, then faded like a song.
She rose up past telephone poles and rooftops of houses where the earth-bound hid.
She rose up sleeker than the sparrows that swirled around her like a jubilant cyclone.
She rose up, confounding Air Traffic Control with her unidentified, tiny red blip.
She rose up and scrunched her toes as though the sky beneath were a fresh-mown lawn.
She rose up and with a swish of her fingers parted storm clouds like a plastic bead curtain.
She rose up, shooting through the ozone with a tangerine shower of sparks.
She rose up past satellites and every cell phone down on earth rang out at once.
She rose up but remembered to politely wave goodbye...
The tide went out for half the world when she gently bumped her head against the moon.
Stars got caught in her weightless, dirty-blond hair.

THEREFORE NEVERTHELESS MOREOVER

but what is more in addition besides
still furthermore likewise & more to the point
yet equally however on the other hand
& in view of that accordingly
then again in contrast
conversely in opposition & in spite of this
hence as a result for that reason
& if so then & consequently
it can be stated to sum up briefly in conclusion
to a degree in part limited so to speak
to a certain extent somewhat fairly
rather relatively reasonably
beyond all equitable dispute
& without undue straining of credibility
with ineluctably unambiguous
& positively inarguable certitude
to be sure without a doubt
I think perhaps
maybe?
I guess I…
I…

um

LOSING HOME

We're driving through my old hometown; I want to show you the house where I was raised. But the A&P is where the library was, and the library is where the armoury was, and the armoury is where the Anglican church once stood. The road becomes a strand of spaghetti. We're on one of thousands of strands, each with a miniature car crawling slowly along it. But the strands are loops and none of us will ever get home. Suddenly the switchback straightens out before us. We are alone and you begin to sing as we barrel down the open road.

COPING WITH THE WAR ON TERROR

for Ron Padgett

Today they took away the tiny man
who lives inside my refrigerator.
(You know, the little guy who
turns the fridge light off and on.)
My neighbour tells me he's
been called an Enemy Combatant.
And though we never met face-to-face
I'm gonna miss that shy little guy.
Now the fridge is always dark.
I can't find my low-fat mayo.

MY THREADBARE BLACK ARMBAND

"Never that which is shall die."
—Euripedes

is is
& always will be is
is will never be was
even when is is was

when is is was
is is is!
& always will be will be
when will be is is
& is was

WISH FULFILLMENT

I sit at a table in a restaurant with the sexy, young Dutch backpacker I booked into the hostel earlier that day. I say restaurant because the table is small and round with a red-checkered tablecloth and a man dressed like an upscale waiter keeps rushing back and forth. But maybe this isn't a restaurant at all but my old childhood bedroom made up to look like a restaurant as though by a lazy and under-funded set dresser. The walls are the same pale blue my bedroom was, with cheap, unconvincing gold-painted sconces tacked up. Beach towels hang there, too, in a pathetic attempt to pass as tapestries, and the food on the plate is obviously plastic. Yes, it is my room: in the corner I see the doorway of the dark closet that used to frighten me so much at night. I turn to the Dutch girl sitting across from me and she leans over and kisses me hard on the lips. We climb onto the table and start undressing each other. As we kiss, a black plume of smoke rises between us from underneath the table. Not really smoke but a viscous, semi-liquid substance. It grows and hardens, pushing us apart. We try to move around it but the smoke creature has become almost solid and keeps matching our movements and blocking our way. The thing turns flesh-coloured, then sprouts clothes and a head of hair. It is my girlfriend from Canada. She smiles and tries to kiss me but I push her back under the table. Then the Dutch girl and I are in a large cave lit with candles on the ground. We are slow-dancing. I am running my fingers through her hair when I realize it is just a blond wig with brown curls hidden underneath. It's my girlfriend dressed up like the Dutch girl to fool me. For the first time I notice she's wearing traditional Dutch clothing complete with wooden shoes—a child's idea of a Dutch girl. I'm angry I was fooled by such a terrible disguise. But then she kisses me and we start undressing each other. I run my fingers through her hair and realize this is also a wig and under it is blond hair. It's the Dutch girl dressed up like my girlfriend. We take off our clothes. I tell her I feel bad doing this because I'm already in a relationship. She explains that she and my girlfriend are really the same person. Of course! I am relieved and suddenly we are floating under-water, locked in each other's arms, breathing in the liquid as though it were air.

THE INCUBATOR SONG

for Alexander

I cannot turn away
my eyes incredulous
my nose pressed up to incubator glass
mottled patches of red and white
beneath your sheath of tissue paper skin
you are a sausage!
6 weeks before your due date &
4lbs. 7 oz. on the butchers scale
a crazy science project of prime ground tubes and wires
crackling deli-meat battery!
your power could light a 100 hospital wards
you make my mouth water
I want to bite you (ever so gently)
on the precise spot where tiny calf
bulges out of lower leg
Mmmmmm!

LIES OF PSYCHOLOGY

how do we reckon the sum of the someone?
the somebodies & nonebodies
the nobodies & yesbodies
the anybodies & manybodies
the thisness of thatness
& usness of them
sure no thing is nothing
& no one is no two
yet even with the ones we love
the loves we won
who will tell us the why of what's what?
when there is no I in Identity?
when even my I is blind to the me
& even myself myother

excerpt from THE GENEALOGY

Bluebottle begat Astronaut.
Astronaut begat Foolscap.
Foolscap begat Arrowhead.
Arrowhead begat Fireman.
Fireman begat Chicken.
Chicken begat Continental Drift.
Continental Drift begat Cornflower.
Cornflower begat Fountain Pen.
Fountain Pen begat Kitten.
Kitten begat Super Nova.
Super Nova begat Bicycle.
Bicycle begat Anger.
Anger begat Candle.
Candle begat Spider Eggs.
Spider Eggs begat Telephone.
Telephone begat Crab.
Crab begat Glass Of Milk.
Glass Of Milk begat Radar.
Radar begat Cocker Spaniel.
Cocker Spaniel begat Infamy.
Infamy begat Toast.
Toast begat Postal Worker.

Postal Worker begat Grain of Sand.
Grain Of Sand begat Gravy.
Gravy begat Leap Year.
Leap Year begat Ocean.
Ocean begat Typewriter.
Typewriter begat Eel.
Eel begat Apple Cider.
Apple Cider begat Plutonium.
Plutonium begat Chewing Gum.
Chewing Gum begat Adultery.
Adultery begat Cheese Grater.
Cheese Grater begat Global Warming.
Global Warming begat Tic-Tac-Toe.
Tic-Tac-Toe begat Horse Hair.
Horse Hair begat Fudge.
Fudge begat Oasis.
Oasis begat Shag Carpet.
Shag Carpet begat Transubstantiation.
Transubstantiation begat Mouse Trap.
Mouse Trap begat Pickle.
Pickle begat Communism.
Communism begat Light Switch.
Light Switch begat Narwhale.
Narwhale begat Nail Bomb.
Nail Bomb begat Tulip.

THE SUN IS DEAD

The room is a perfect white cube without window or door. From the high ceiling hangs an electric wire that ends in a light bulb. It casts a harsh white glare down on everything. A small bearded man is tied to a chair, the only furniture in the room. His face is covered with fresh red marks and old, dark purple ones surrounded by yellow. He is extremely agitated. My partner is shouting things at the suspect like, "WHO TOOK THE BIG BLUE SKY FROM THE WANDERING PLATYPUS?" It is an old interrogation technique we call "Alice In Wonderland." We spout nothing but gibberish at the suspect for days on end. At first he laughs at us. After a few days he gets angry. Then he gets very quiet. Finally he starts trying to make sense of what we're saying, reading hidden meanings into all the blather. Here he often begins to slip up, revealing valuable information. Right now the suspect is silent, simmering, but he will crack in the next few minutes. I shout, "THE SUN IS DEAD! THE SUN IS DEAD! THE SUN IS DEAD!" and punctuate each sentence with a slap across the suspect's mouth, drawing blood. Suddenly he is telling us everything he knows: the names of the members of his cell, the identities of his superiors, the names of moles in our organization. I know he is telling the truth because we already have all this information; my job was simply to get him to admit it. After he signs the confession he smiles at us. There is not a tooth left in his head. In the hallway outside my partner is effusive, praising my technique. How I knew just what to do to break the suspect. How I am a credit to the organization. I grab my partner by the collar and my fist flashes outward. His nose collapses with a crunch.

HOME IN MY POCKET

there is a little here
in every there
there is a little here
in everywhere
a hence in thence
a hither in thither
& wherever wherever is
here will be there

SPADINA FOOD MARKET

SPADINA OPEN
F 7DAYS
O A WEEK
O
D
—
M
A
R
T

OPEN

LIVE LONG
DRINK WATER
CHEAP CHEAP
SMOKES POP
MILK SNACKS

Coca-Cola
2 LITRE
$ 1.79

SPADINA FOOD MARKET

GAMES FOR THE YOUNG AND YOUNG AT HEART

One of you plays lumberjack. The rest pretend to be trees. One by one the lumberjack cuts down all the trees. The game is over when the last tree is cut down and the lumberjack suffocates on his own carbon dioxide.

Choose a common household object. Hold it up and tell a make-believe story about how it is evidence of the manufacture of weapons of mass destruction. The more far-fetched the explanation the better. Use your imagination!

"Upper and Lower House": Everyone lies down in an area called "The Lower House" and pretends that they are dead. The person who can play dead the longest wins and is admitted to "The Upper House" where they get to do nothing for the rest of their lives until they really are dead!

Split up into two teams. Half of you must act like Government Agents and the other half like Terrorists. Try to guess the difference!

Game for kids in New York. One person builds a house out of a cardboard box and tries to make a meal from kitchen leftovers in the garbage. Another person known as "The Mayor" kicks that person until they beg for mercy. Then he kicks them some more.

Take a pair of scissors, a bowl and a needle and thread. Perform a self-appendectomy. This game is called "Two-Tier Healthcare."

Game for 33 million people. Choose one of you to be Prime Minister. The Prime Minister stands in the corner blindfolded and waits for someone to tell him what to do. (That's the game. It never ends. There are no winners.)

SIGNS OF CONNECTION

"ampersand—n. the sign & (=and).
[corrup. of and per se and ('&' by itself is 'and')]"
—Oxford Encyclopedic English Dictionary

ampersand
is two ands
two ands within an &
an and & an and
an and and in &

I find this very interesting

DEGENERATE MYOPIA: after Oedipus, Samson & Tiresias

20/200	E	61.0 M	1
20/100	A C	30.5 M	2
20/70	H S T	21.3 M	3
20/50	R I P M	15.2 M	4
20/40	O R E U N	12.2 M	5
20/30	F O C U S E	9.14 M	6
20/25	D T I L D I S	7.62 M	7
20/20	T A N C E R E N	6.10 M	8
20/15	E R S T H E M I	4.57 M	9
20/13	N D I S T I N C T	3.96 M	10
20/10	T O T H E N A K E D I	3.05 M	11

ANOTHER DEAD IRAQI

End of a long, hard day
of being himself,
The President prepares for sleep.
Enters the bedroom.
Looks up.
Frowns.
Another dead Iraqi in his bed!
Sunni, Shiite, or Kurd.
Who can tell?
He picks up the phone.
Pauses.
Forgets.
Should he call Security
or Housekeeping?

HIPPIE BATH DAY

for John

too bothers Jinn & Muck identifull twains
accelerate the teenth anti-versity of therr naive-tivity
with a beliefull of won cake betwixt the too twains
onely years hince would t(hey!) kevetchous
be dessertirous of the duo-cake after Muck's growlfriend
indictated the new(mmm)error-kill discrapency
Sandy wizz there pooh-lite & salivized
& Gary Satler rupt the coff uff my sheert
whand wee h(id) be/hint the C-owch
frum havey-browed best-fiend Joey Dowdy
who invated hisself whiff hiss non-envy-tation
& oop on the screem the supper-ate feel'em projactor
projacted a kertoom Chilly Willy that F-unny arktic burr'd
hee wuzz allwizz ether coold or hungreed
& so! F-unny wee hee-h(awed)
till it wuzz (OH!)ver & everybuddy cr(eye)d

METAPHOR

The poet is searching for a metaphor, cursing himself for letting his supply run thin. He scratches his head in bewilderment and out drops an old metaphor that was lodged behind his right ear. It lies on the desk before him, smelling slightly like mildewed wood. He doesn't remember putting it behind his ear but he is a poet and organization is not one of his strong points. The metaphor looks like a dove or a heart or a star or some such thing. It's so old and beaten up it seems as if at any second it's going to completely fall apart. He throws it in the trash can and continues his search.

He rummages through the things on his desk: sunglasses, day-timer, telephone, pens, pencils, books, papers. Could any of these be a metaphor? Metaphors are tricky. They often look like everyday objects. In fact some of the best metaphors are things that don't draw attention to themselves at all, like a Styrofoam cup or a supermarket trolley. He sees a paperclip. Is this not only a paperclip but also the metaphor he's been looking for? He tries out "Life's Cruel Paperclip." Can he use this? Probably couldn't write a whole poem around it, but since it is only a very small metaphor he slips it into his pocket for future use.

The poet has not really run out of metaphors. He has just run out of good ones. He has whole closets full of dead metaphors, broken-down metaphors cluttering his garage, faulty metaphors gathering dust in the basement. His wife has been bothering him to sell them or just throw the damn things out but he is reluctant. "Time's Winged Chariot," "A Sea of Troubles," "The Bloom of Youth." He has been collecting them from the moment he began to talk. He didn't know he was going to be a poet back then, one whose stock in trade was metaphor. It was just something he did. These metaphors had the heft and weight of real objects, but if cracked open they proved to be nothing more than hollow shells. An egg that had become a metaphor long ago but died from overuse was worthless, fit neither for writing a poem nor for making an omelet. And the poet didn't have just one or two dozen of these dead metaphors; he had thousands.

He walked over to one of his piles of old metaphors. If only he could find some use for them. An antique side table with four spindly legs lay abandoned in the middle of the heap. He knew at one time, long ago, these spindles had been named "legs" because of perceived similarities to human legs; they too were long and thin, "stood" upright and held up the table in much the same way legs hold up the human body. But at some point in history people became inured to the original meaning of the metaphor and the leg in "table leg" was lost from view. The metaphor was dead, a mere word.

Yet the poet remembered too that during the nineteenth century "leg," with its associations of an intimate human body part, had suddenly become alive again to the scandalized Victorians. So they invented tablecloths to cover these unseemly legs just as a skirt covers a woman's. Of course time passed and the metaphor died once again. But that did not change one unalterable fact: if the leg metaphor was once dead but managed (for a while) to be revivified then no metaphor is ever truly dead. At any given moment it can be resuscitated so that we once again see the original metaphor in all its living glory.

The poet was excited. He pulled the table out of the pile and placed it in the centre of the room. Then, at the top of his lungs he shouted, "The table legs danced a jig!" And, indeed, the table legs began to dance, wheeling around the poet, delighted to be alive once more. The poet had his metaphor at last.

MAN OF STEEL

Playing in the tree fort
with best friend Steven Turner,
I suddenly turn to him and shout,
"Look! I'm Superman!"
and launch my tiny body, arms outstretched,
sail into empty air,
hang there a moment,
then come crashing down belly-first
onto the edge of the sandbox.

It knocks the wind clear out of me.
I lie there like I'm dead.
A thousand radiating points of pain.
Steven yells for our mothers
who come running frantically,
and ask: "What on earth happened?"
And without the least hesitation,
I point my finger at my friend
and say, "Steven pushed me!"

As Steven's mother whacks
the backside of her child
without mercy, ignoring
his protests of innocence,
I barely notice, I am so amazed
that for one brief moment,
I was the Man Of Steel.
That nothing could harm me.
That I could fly.

TXT MSGS 2 MRCL DCHMP

A SAGGING LANDSCAPE WAS HIS GUT. HIS LAZINESS COULD BEND THE HANDS OF CLOCKS.

THE CIRCLE WAS ROUND LIKE A SQUARE.

THE SNAKE FALLS IN LOVE WITH THE NECKLACE.

DEFINITION OF AN ELOQUENT PERSON: SOMEONE WHO CAN DESCRIBE A SPIRAL STAIRCASE WITHOUT USING HIS HANDS.

HOLD THIS POEM UP TO YOUR EAR AND YOU WILL HEAR THE SOUND OF THE SEA—A SEA MADE OF CRINKLING PAPER.

THE NOTE

For a moment I am blinded by the bright halogen lights from above. I shield my eyes and look around. I'm in an operating theatre fraught with commotion, people talking excitedly amongst themselves. A five-year-old black girl with cornrows lies anesthetized on the table in front of me. An abdominal incision held open with clamps reveals the interior of her stomach. People in green gowns and surgical masks are shouting at me, "Doctor, what should we do?" But I don't know what to do. There is something white lodged in the cavity of her stomach. I reach in, pull out a small piece of paper, unfold it. It is a handwritten note but the writing is smeared and illegible. I had hoped it would tell me how to save the girl.

I am in a bar, I think in Amsterdam, though everyone here, the customers and waitresses, is speaking perfect English. I realize they are doing it for my benefit, to make me feel less of a stranger in this strange town and I am touched. I am just about to sip my pint when a beautiful woman with striking blond hair smiles at me from across the aisle. She has the loveliest skin I've ever seen: milk chocolate. We can't stop looking at each other. Without a word I join her at her table. We lean in closer. The air in front of her face thickens to a gossamer veil, yet through the distortion her skin grows only more luminous. We both feel a moment of giddy vertigo as we stare across the tiny, infinite chasm of inches that lies between us. We waver a moment at the edge before finally, irrevocably, surrendering to the pull, free-falling slowly into each other's soft, waiting lips.

The patio of another bar: another time, another place. In the background the mountains turn violet as the sun sets behind them. I tell her this will never work, this thing between us. She is upset but hides it well. Her skin is now white and freckled, her hair a violent red. I continue to talk and look up again; her skin is ashen, her hair jet black. Next she is brown-haired with a tan. She is every girlfriend I have ever had and this breakup will hurt as badly as if I'd broken up with all of them at once. She says she will never give up on us being together.

A man glares at me across the empty discotheque. We are the only customers. I know if I don't leave immediately he will do something violent. Suddenly I realize he is the husband of my girlfriend and he knows everything. I slam down my half-finished drink, dash out of the room down a broad winding staircase. I run with long, loping strides, three steps at a time. He is right behind me, corners me and backs me into a wall. I scuttle up the wall backwards, my feet and hands somehow finding purchase in the tiny ledges of jutting mortar between the bricks. I am thirty feet off the floor clinging to the wall when he tries to leap up and grab me. He lands on the ground and I drop off the wall down on top of him, knocking him unconscious. I steal his shoes and run out into the street.

My girlfriend, her young daughter and I have just finished a ride on a roller coaster and are standing on the exit platform. My girlfriend turns her back and I quickly scribble a note on a piece on paper telling her it's over for good. I hand the note to the girl and whisper, "Give this to your mother." She giggles, running fingers over her cornrows, puts the note in her mouth and swallows.

THE SQUATTERS OF DIDDLY

i. Paperclip the Moon

Yammering flibbertigibbet!
Eternal isness of the yes's no.
The never very much of ever such.
Dance me the 2-step Cha-cha.
Posi-nega-whatsit?
A conga line of Tuesdays.
For "rectitude" please read "rectilinear".
Roger dodger under & out.

ii. Toodeloo

To be a Fly on the Wal—
dorf salad when the Shinola hits the Fan—
dango! And Everything is coming up Ro—
sez you. Yeah, the pish on your Ed is just Wayne...

NURSERY BOOK CONFIDENTIAL

for Bill Knott

Humpty Dumpty was a jumper.
Jacky Paper freaked on acid.
Gretel got away with murder.
Big Bad Wolf was framed.
Cinderella? One more gold-digger—
Charming screwed her two stepsisters.
Little Bo Peep got hooked on crack.
Punch is on restraining orders.
Chicken Little's in a psych ward.
Sleeping Beauty's had a facelift.
The Tortoise won his race on 'roids.
The Dish left the Spoon for a Placemat.
And Old MacDonald lost the farm. I-O I-O-U

5 O'CLOCK MONDAY MORNING THE ALARM CLOCK RINGS

the wave throws itself bodily on the rocks
is dashed to tiny pieces
pauses
lets out a sigh
then wearily pulls its pieces
back together again
scurries into the sea's waiting arms
where it sits there gathering courage
waiting for re-enforcements
before assaulting the rocks once again

ERNST JANDL COUNTS UP TO ZEHN ON BOTH HÄNDE

three eight

zer0

sechs vier

eine

neun seven

fünf

zwei ten!

MIST

Standing in the hallway of a Victorian house, I place my hand on the wooden banister of a narrow winding staircase. The banister is suspended by spindles carved with Chinese dragons intricately entwined. As I slowly ascend the stairs the air becomes thick with bees. Each bee wears a pair of miniature World War One fighter pilot goggles. The bees are talking to each other over radios. The squawking of their high-pitched voices and the buzzing of their wings is deafening. They begin to assemble mid-flight into various holding patterns. The patterns are letters of the alphabet. The bees are trying to spell out a message for me but they are slow, confused. By the time they've formed a letter I've forgotten the letter that went before it. I reach the top of the stairs and look at the ceiling. Just below it, tiny storm clouds are forming. The bees are all gone save one that preens itself on a fan-shaped stained-glass window. A loud rumble from the little clouds shakes the house. Then it begins to rain. Raindrops so small they feel like mist on my hands and face.

THE FLOWERS OF MT. PLEASANT

"Death and the sun are not to be looked at steadily."
—Francois Duc de la Rochefoucauld

One day,
Fine.
All fine.
You & everyone you love—
Fine.
One spring day.

Then one day,
Dead.
All dead.
You & everyone you love—
Dead.
One spring day.

THEN I DEFY YOU, STARS*

*disasterisk

THE NEXT GREAT DINER CATACLYSM

for Stuart Ross

The diner's hungry morning crowd, oblivious as slaughterhouse chickens. I go to the broom closet where my new computer terminal constantly downloads petabytes of multiple data streams: seismic readings, weight thresholds, barometric pressure, combustibility, tensile strength and a thousand other variables that might predict the next great diner cataclysm.

Last week The Terrible Toothpick Brushfire left the patrons with blackened faces and strands of chicken salad still lodged between their teeth. Two days later The Diet Coke Deluge flooded the place with sputtering, sticky patrons lying scattered in its wake. And who could forget last month's Black Hole Pudding, devouring everything that came within its awesome gravitational pull. The woman who ordered it lost all her hairpins, her two favourite earrings and needed a week off work to "recover emotionally."

Remember being snowed in for days and running out of gravy in The Instant Mash Potato Blizzard of 2007? And The Frightful Sparkling Waterspouts with their chilling carbonated spray? The thousands of matchbooks wasted in the fight against The Wobbly Tables Earthquake?

I survey the scene of this recent devastation, walk among the tables of innocents. I am all present tense, muscles taut as hydro cables. It's quiet. Too quiet. Something is terribly wrong. Suddenly I hear a rumble from above. And then at the last instant, I move to my left and deftly sidestep a Deadly Avalanche of Scrambled Eggs!

No one hurt, thank God. At least for now we're safe. But for how long? Back at my desk the dark whirlpool that sleeps inside my coffee cup churns restlessly.

THE FATHER WITH THREE DIFFERENT BRAINS

for Stephen

The father looks at the baby.
The baby is crying.
Should he pick up the child?
The father's three different brains debate what to do.

The cerebral cortex argues one shouldn't reward
this behaviour; it leads to dependency.
The mammalian brain wants to comfort the child, feel its warmth.
The father's reptilian brain wants to *eat the baby.*

It is a three-way deadlock...
The father looks at the baby.
The baby is crying.

ON THE TRAIL OF THE EDIBLE SMITHEE

:)
:)
:)
:)
:)
:)
:)
:)
:):):):):):):):):):):):)**FUCKYOU**:):):):):):):):):):):):)
:)
:)
:)
:)
:)
:)
:)
:)

from EULOGY FOR CITY LIFE

This town
has wolfed us down
like bad meat, our protests
a rumble in the pit of its
stomach.

❧

Angry
down to our bones,
we do violence to the
day—our shadows punch holes in the
sunlight.

❧

Metal
shutters lid the
city's sleeping eyes. I
want to ask her, does she only
dream us?

LITTLE SUN, O LITTLE SUN

for Emma

Little Sun, O Little Sun, are you in love with me?
It seems whenever I turn around you're there.
In the morning as soon as you get up out of bed
you go straight to my bedroom window,
tickling my face with your warm, golden fingers.
And when I go to school you are there
pulling my pigtails, blaming class clown Jimmy.
When I play tag at recess you dog my every step,
dancing around my feet like a love-sick puppy.
And when I go to sleep you go to sleep, too,
mooning for me sadly all night long.
Little Sun, O Little Sun, you *are* in love with me.
Silly fellow. A girl can't marry the sun!

THE ANNEXATION

Picket fences
goosestep over marshland.
Name their new protectorate
Sunny Glade Subdivision.

ELLIPTICAL

"...a lost child's trail of fairy tale bread crumbs...the stars of Orion's Belt...the final Morse code message from the bridge of a gutted ship...the maddening secrets of a crumbling papyrus...a tortoise laying her eggs on the beach...the street urchin's first sign of small pox...the distant approach lights of a fog-choked runway...all the words that stay unspoken simply being understood..."

THE FOUR SAY-SO'S

i. SPRUNG!

The blue's all sparrowed up.
The peaceful natters riverly.
Cedarish, the swaying.
Cattish, the fence.
The garden? Pure tulipian.
Everything is sundayful.

ii. SIMMER,

You skip across the water's surface like a stone
suddenly freed from its own heavy thoughts.
Me plodding along the beach beside you,
a city still strapped to my back.
Seagulls burrow tunnels in air.
Your hair is a dirty-blond breeze.
Mist encircles the rock
as your lips encircle my name.
Water rushes up to kiss you,
sun, embrace you
and you linger there to let them do so.
Sands beneath your feet
spilt from a broken hourglass.

iii. FELL.

Fly away, Scarecrow! Let the crows roost.
Fall back! Fall back! You Army of Hours.
Heaven's closed up shop with shutters of steel.
Leaves hemorrhage spectrums and trees explode.

These are the months that rhyme with "remember".
Crumbling mementos of girls named April or May.
Time flicks his finger and nights fall like dominos.
The harvest moon swells like a rotted peach.

iv. WITHER?

The slumbering Earth abandons the fight
and buries her face in a pillow of snow.
She will not wake up
though clouds, tubercular, cough up blizzards
and fanatical winds holler angry rants.
Here life turns inward, exists as pure potential.
A dream of what this world could be—
a world where hope is green
and birds convert St. Francis.
April-starved habitué of frost-spangled windows,
quit your snow-blind gazing—look within.
The thing you seek is a seed inside you.
Springtime is already here.

THE GLASS HOUSE

The owner of The Glass House shakes my hand, invites me in. His palm is delicate and cold. I scan the cozy interior and wonder how The Glass House got its name; it seems like a typical family home. The man says, "It is difficult living here—the walls, floors and ceilings all look normal but are actually made entirely of glass and all the rooms are filled with glass furniture as well. Even so much as a loud noise could cause the whole thing to come crashing down, killing us all." He motions to me to sit down on the couch, cautioning me to be gentle. I slowly sink into it and am surprised at how soft and natural it feels despite being made of glass. All the while the man shuffles around in padded slippers and barely talks above a whisper. He tells me he never leaves the house for fear that harm may come to his family and home if he is not here to stand guard. A beautiful woman enters the room. The man introduces her as his wife. He hears a low groaning noise coming from deep within the house and excuses himself to investigate. I say to the woman, "This must be quite stressful." She leans in and whispers, "The house isn't really made of glass. It is my husband who is made of glass. We had to lie to him. This way he feels that he is protecting us and because he is so careful, he never harms himself." The man returns and I notice the red of his dress shirt is actually blood flowing beneath a paper-thin sheath of glass. "False alarm," he says and grins.

ACKNOWLEDGEMENTS

Some of these poems have appeared previously (often in different incarnations) in literary publications both in print and online. A big "Thank you!" to the editors at *Kiss Machine* ("Man Of Steel", "Losing Home", "The Note"), *Misunderstandings* ("Spadina Food Market", "TXT MSGS 2 MRL DCHMP", "Therefore Nevertheless Moreover"), *The New Chief Tongue* ("Ernst Jandl Counts Up To Zehn On Both Hände"), *Other Cl/utter* e-zine and *Other Cl/utter: An Andthology* ("On The Trail Of The Edible Smithee"), and *Rampike* ("My Threadbare Black Armband", "Mist", "The Genealogy", "Degenerate Myopia"). "Here There Everywhere", (now called "Home In My Pocket") was commissioned by Wm. Whiteley Ltd., a wayfinding and design company, to celebrate their 30th anniversary. Thanks, Bill.

Kudos to Stuart Ross for his excellent editorial suggestions. Thanks to the staff at Coach House for another great production job. Bravo Krista Ellis for taking a fine author's photo. Also greatly appreciated—the Plasticine Collective and Expressionists workshops, where many of these poems made their first public appearances.

I owe a great debt to those who have continued to help and encourage me as well as my work over the years. Foremost among them, my family, who have never failed me. All my love.

Finally, this book would not exist without my partner, Kristin, the designer of this book, my dirty-blond muse, and the first and most important audience for all these poems.

Photo: Krista Ellis

Mike Freeman was raised in Dundas, Ontario and received a BA from University of Toronto and an MPhil from Trintiy College Dublin. His poetry has been published in numerous magazines, literary journals and e-zines across Canada. Featured in many reading series and literary festivals in Toronto and throughout Ontario, he has also appeared on *Bravo! News*, *Speaker's Corner* and TVO's *Imprint*. His first book of poems, ***Cigarette Salad***, was released in 2006. He currently hosts a popular weekly reading series, ***Bibliopunk Poetry Podcast***, available on iTunes or at his on-line home www.bibliopunk.com. In addition to poetry, he also writes fiction and screenplays. He lives in Toronto. ***Bones*** is his second full-length book.